Teach us to War Righteous Warfare 101

Teach us to War Righteous Warfare 101

Are You Ready for Victory?

Shardell Martin

Shardell Martin

Copyright © 2022 by Shardell Martin
All rights reserved. No part of this book may be reproduced in any manner whatsoever without written permission except in the case of brief quotations embodied in critical articles and reviews

First Printing 2022
Teach us to War: Righteous Warfare 101/ Shardell Martin

ISBN
978-1-7378760-3-8
978-1-7378760-1-4

Shardellmartin.com
Facebook & Instagram: @ Shardell Martin
Email: shardellmartinmin@outlook.com

Unless otherwise stated, all Scriptures is taken from King James Version

To: The Readers

Read responsible. This book is not for everybody and those who read with the wrong intentions may your eyes and ears be closed from receiving the mysteries of the Kingdom of God. This book will have to be read multiple times and at different times or seasons of your life to get all this book has to offer. This is not just a good read but it's for the edifying, preparing and apply to your life as a believer of Jesus Christ. Removing pride is a must when reading this book for God to reveal and pour into you. *And said, Verily I say unto you, except ye be converted, and become as little children, ye shall not enter into the kingdom of heaven* **Matthew 18:3.**

Table of Content:
Chapter 1
Righteous Warfare 101: Are you ready to war?

Chapter 2
Holiness: Offense and Defense

Chapter 3
Build and War

Chapter 4
Part 1: What's your Weapon of Choice?
Part 2: Using your weapons the Right way

Chapter 5
Let's War: it's war time

5

Righteous Warfare 101: Are You Ready to War?

Weapons of Warfare

What are weapons of warfare? **Weapons**: something designed or used to bring harm. **Warfare:** the payment of conflict, battle, or a fight between opposing sides. Weapons of warfare are weapons God gives or have given us to win battles against the kingdom of darkness and for the expanding of the Kingdom of God. **Kingdom of God**: The Lordship/ reign and rule of God thru the inward working of the Holy Spirit in a person. The rule of God, His word, and Holy Spirit in people or areas/territory. **Kingdom of darkness**: the rulership and reign of Satan through demonic forces; evil spirits seeking to gain rule over territories whether thru people, geographical, mentally, emotional, spiritual realm, positions, etc.

This is not the typical teaching about warfare, this is to teach you how to war and win the righteous way according to God. Righteousness will be emphasized because there are rules that govern the Spirit and Natural/ earth realms. To be effective God's way, one must follow His rules. Satan is good at his job because he knows the rules and how to use it against the believers. However now is the time for the believers and followers of Jesus Christ to learn the rules that we may fulfill the original mandate of God : **Genesis 1: 26-27** *26 And God said, Let us* *make man in our image, after our likeness: and let them have dominion over the fish of the sea, and over the fowl of the air, and over the cattle, and over all the earth, and over every creeping thing that creepeth upon the earth.27 So God created man in his own image, in the image of God created he him; male and female created he them.*

No more being passive or reactive, but the time is now to be proactive in taking back what God has given to us as His people. *And from the days of John the Baptist until now, the Kingdom of Heaven suffereth violence, and the violent take it by force* **Matthew 11:12.** No more being wimps. **Wimps**: a weak or cowardly person; fail to do something as a result of fear or lack of confidence. God has designed us to be Conquerors (*Nay, in all these things we are more than conquerors through him that loved us.* **Romans 8:37**) Overcomers (*For whatsoever is born of God overcometh the world: and this is the victory that overcometh the world, even our faith.* **1John 5:4**) Victorious (*But thanks be to God, which giveth us the victory through our Lord Jesus Christ.* **1Corinthians 15:57**) and more, so we have no excuses. If you ready to walk in dominion, inheritance, and being all who God has destined you to be, keep reading. The time is Now for a Kingdom of God Take Over and we are taking what's ours!

Steps to prepare for Warfare

When it comes to doing it right (God's way) and being effective, your lifestyle matters. It will even help you or hurt you. Being **righteous**: Doing things God's way. Is not about being man definition of **perfect**: without mistakes or flaws, but what's the posture of a person heart before God. This is not the time to be religious but the time to be in right standing with God. Meaning how do God see me and my life/ way I live? Man, or people can tell you you're Good but if God not saying you(are) good, than you're not good. In other words, man's opinion or interpretation of you does not matter before God, so you have to make sure you're right with God personally. Not I go to church, I'm a Christian, your title, how long you think you been saved, you tithe, I'm a good person, I pray etc. That don't matter if God see's your heart and lifestyle as being dirty or not right. If you know or want to get right with God here is a prayer to help start you on the right track with God, but it doesn't stop here some changes have to be made on the inside and outside (lifestyle, things you do, etc.)

Say this prayer of repentance with sincerity and you will be on your way to a new start or alignment with God.

Lord, I acknowledge that I need your help, that my life is out of alignment with you and I'm in the wrong and I want to get right with you and to where you want me to be in Jesus' name, I pray amen.

Heavenly Father, I thank you for all those who was led into repentance that you cover and shield them from evil, give those who need a new start a new beginning, those who need to be realign or algin to you and your will for their life to do it for them, I ask that you fill them with your Spirit and let them feel your presence. Do that what needs to be done in their life to align them to your will, and purpose for their life and let them know their change has come in Jesus mighty name I thank you and seal this prayer, Amen. Your change is now and it's more to come 😊

6

Holiness: Offense and Defense

Holy: being pure in heart, motive and intent before God. Set apart by truth and dedicated to God's purpose.

Holiness: the state or place of being holy or pure in heart before God. Holiness is a topic many misunderstand. It has been measured by outward appearance and what I can or cannot do causing many to be misled and go astray from God. Wherever you currently stand spiritually before God, it's important to look to God and allow Him to show you where you need to be perfected in your heart and holiness. *Having therefore these promises, dearly beloved, let us cleanse ourselves from all filthiness of the flesh and spirit, perfecting holiness in the fear of God.* **2 Corinthians 7:1**. We all have room for growth, no time for being prideful or in denial because God is going to be perfecting us until the time of Christ return. *Being confident of this very thing, that he which hath begun a good work in you will perform it until the day of Jesus Christ*: **Philippians 1:6**. It's ok to need God's help, but it's not ok to need it and do not get it.

When it comes to warfare holiness is a **defense:** The action of protecting or resisting attack; and **offense**: the action of attacking or assaulting someone or something. Holiness allows you to do both at the same time against the enemy. When we submitted to God, holiness gives us the power to resist the devil and make him flee (*Submit yourselves therefore to God. Resist the devil, and he will flee from you.* **James 4:7**). Holiness grants access to high realms in God, the ability to fly above the storms of life, the ability to abide in God's presence, allows God to move on your behalf, command things / decree and more. Holiness allows us to be able to effectively war and do damage against the kingdom of darkness. (1 *He that dwelleth in the secret place of the most High shall abide under the shadow of the Almighty. 2 I will say of the Lord, He is my refuge and my fortress: my God; in him will I trust. 3 Surely, he shall deliver thee from the snare of the fowler, and from the noisome pestilence. 4 He shall cover thee with his feathers, and under his wings shalt thou trust: his truth shall be thy shield and buckler. 5 Thou shalt not be afraid for the terror by night; nor for the arrow that flieth by day; 6 Nor for the pestilence that walketh in darkness; nor for the destruction that wasteth at noonday. 7 A thousand shall fall at thy side, and ten thousand at thy right hand; but it shall not come nigh thee. 8 Only with thine eyes shalt thou behold and see the reward of the wicked. 9 Because thou hast made the Lord, which is my refuge, even the most High, thy habitation; 10 There shall no evil befall thee, neither shall any plague come nigh thy dwelling. 11 For he shall give his angels charge over thee, to keep thee in all thy ways. 12 They shall bear thee up in their hands, lest thou dash thy foot against a stone.* **Psalms 91:1-12.** So next time you go to spiritual warfare remember there is power in holiness, so do not go without the weapon of holiness.

7

Build and War

When God calls or choose you for His purpose, you're being picked to build and war For His Kingdom. With this comes warfare from God opposing enemy Satan and his kingdom of darkness. There's two main ways Satan seek to stop us, through personal attacks and purpose assigned attacks. Meaning personal warfare are attacks against you such as: **physically and Socially**: health, desires of your flesh, relationships, character, your past and so on. **Occupationally**: career, school, poverty, finance, and so on. **Mentally**: mindset, your will, way you think, strongholds, generational curses and so on. **Emotionally**: making you think what you feel is real, rejection, abandonment, not being properly loved and so on and **Spiritually:** your relationship with God, obedience, submission, your purpose/ call and so on. The other is assignment/ purpose assigned. Meaning warfare that comes to attack or stop the assignment/ purpose of God from being done. Satan know in order to be successful in stopping the will of God from being done, he must get you to be in-effective in one of the two. A person cannot be successful in neither without being successful in both. Example one can right now be doing something God purposed them to do but if you not doing it from the place of being in God image/ who God destined you to be then you're not most effective in the call/ purpose. Don't be fooled by the results it's nowhere near what God destined and intended for you.

Just because Satan wants to stop it doesn't mean he wins or will. This is a fixed fight God wins. God equips us to teach us how to win, not lose. The only way you lose is if you don't fight. This chapter is to prepare you mentally and emotionally for the warfare. Often, we set out to go to war/ work the purpose of God for our life and we expect everything to go well. It's ok to expect for it to be accomplished but not for there to be no opposition, it comes with this in many ways. Again, this is to prepare you because for *God hath not given us a spirit of fear; but of power, and of love and of a sound mind* **2Timothy 1:7**. It's time to be sound in our mind and thinking. **Sound:** entire; unbroken not shaky split or defective. To expect to go to war/fulfill your purpose and there be no counterattack is childish, ignorant, and naive thinking. It's ok for it to come so you can get the victory but it's not ok for it to stay or win. No warfare, opposition, doubt, fear, unbelief, lies, persecution, betrayal, slander, losing people and so on will not overpower you or take you down. Casualties comes with this. How can you have victories, be an overcomer, conqueror and so on if there is no opposition? You're not just a civilian / average or just anybody. You been enlisted, called or chosen by God to be a supernatural being, created by a winner, who never loses, to do supernatural things and win supernatural wars. Armor up we are going to war your general (God) has called you, are you ready to report for duty? Your assignment: be ready to build and war!

Example of being ready to build and war

Nehemiah is a great example of a servant of the Lord who was ready to build and war.

1 But it came to pass, that when Sanballat heard that we builded the wall, he was wroth, and took great indignation, and mocked the Jews. 2 And he spake before his brethren and the army of Samaria, and said, What do these feeble Jews? will they fortify themselves? will they sacrifice? will they make an end in a day? will they revive the stones out of the heaps of the rubbish which are burned? 3 Now Tobiah the Ammonite was by him, and he said, Even that which they build, if a fox go up, he shall even break down their stone wall. 4 Hear, O our God; for we are despised: and turn their reproach upon their own head, and give them for a prey in the land of captivity: 5 And cover not their iniquity, and let not their sin be blotted out from before thee: for they have provoked thee to anger before the builders. 6 So built we the wall; and all the wall was joined together unto the half thereof: for the people had a mind to work. 7 But it came to pass, that when Sanballat, and Tobiah, and the Arabians, and the Ammonites, and the Ashdodites, heard that the walls of Jerusalem were made up, and that the breaches began to be stopped, then they were very wroth, 8 And conspired all of them together to come and to fight against Jerusalem, and to hinder it. 9 Nevertheless we made our prayer unto our God, and set a watch against them day and night, because of them. 10 And Judah said, The strength of the bearers of burdens is decayed, and there is much rubbish; so that we are not able to build the wall. 11 And our adversaries said, They shall not know, neither see, till we come in the midst among them, and slay them, and cause the work to cease. 12 And it came to pass, that when the Jews which dwelt by them came, they said unto us ten times, From all places whence ye shall return unto us they will be upon you. 13 Therefore set I in the lower places behind the wall, and on the higher places, I even set the people after their families with their swords, their spears, and their bows. 14 And I looked, and rose up, and said unto the nobles, and to the rulers, and to the rest of the people, Be not ye afraid of them: remember the Lord, which is great and terrible, and fight for your brethren, your sons, and your daughters, your wives, and your houses. 15 And it came to pass, when our enemies heard that it was known unto us, and God had brought their counsel to nought, that we returned all of us to the wall, every one unto his work. 16 And it came to pass from that time forth, that the half of my servants wrought in the work, and the other half of them held both the spears, the shields, and the bows, and the habergeons; and the rulers were behind all the house of Judah. 17 They which builded on the wall, and they that bare burdens, with those that laded, every one with one of his hands wrought in the work, and with the other hand held a weapon. 18 For the builders, every one had his sword girded by his side, and so builded. And he that sounded the trumpet was by me. 19 And I said unto the nobles, and to the rulers, and to the rest of the people, The work is great and large, and we are separated upon the wall, one far from another. 20 In what place therefore ye hear the sound of the trumpet, resort ye thither unto us: our God shall fight for us. 21 So we laboured in the work: and half of them held the spears from the rising of the morning till the stars appeared. 22 Likewise at the same time said I unto the people, Let every one with his servant lodge within Jerusalem, that in the night they may be a guard to us, and labour on the day. 23 So neither I, nor my brethren, nor my servants, nor the men of the guard which followed me, none of us put off our clothes, saving that every one put them off for washing. **Nehemiah 6: 1-23**

Here are some of the lessons I want to point out from these verses.

Verses 1-3 lesson: brace yourself. Be prepared for when those who are not in agreement with you or what you are doing to come up against you. Whether it's with their words, actions, and getting others to join their cause to come against you.

Verse 4 lesson: when people come up against you in the natural/flesh. You respond in the Spirit by turning to God and praying. This is not a flesh war (he/ she did something to me so I'm going to do something back) you will lose that way. *For we wrestle not against flesh and blood, but against principalities, against powers, against the rulers of the darkness of this world, against spiritual wickedness in high places.* **Ephesians 6:12**

Verse 5 lesson: it's important to watch one mouth because you can think you speaking against a person or the work, they do without realizing you are speaking against God, because it was God who sent them to do the work not themselves. God will protect what He builds and who He send. *Except the Lord build the house, they labour in vain that build it: except the Lord keep the city, the watchman waketh but in vain* **Psalm 127:1.**

Verse 6- 14 & 20-23 lesson: the opposition comes to strengthen you. Because they came against Israel it made Nehemiah see where they were weak at and as a result, they got on guard to not just build but now war spiritually, strengthen themselves, pray to God and get strategy. They started watching and praying, got their weapons, trumpets to sound for when the enemy come so the other can be alerted where to come and fight, they set up watchmen, mentally prepared (they did not take their clothes off), and everything else they needed to complete the assignment.

Verse 15 lesson: because the Lord was with them, He allowed them to hear the plan their enemies were making for them. They looked to God and followed the instructions and made themselves ready for war. Then God brought their enemies plan to naught/ nothing, meaning it did not work.

Verse 16- 23 lesson: It's a great work God called you to so know who's on your team and protect the work. Keep your weapon with you even when it seems like the warfare back up or stopped, stay ready. Don't give the enemy no room to get in or attack.

Let people do and say what they want, it's ok because God is fighting for you. *What shall we then say to these things? If God be for us, who can be against us?* **Romans 8:31** So instead of entertaining the distractions make yourself ready for war and keep building.

8

Part 1: What's your Weapon of Choice?

A soldier does not go to war without his weapon and a General is always armed. What is your weapon of choice? Is it the clapping of hands, Praise, worship, praying or speaking the word of God, walking the floor, love, fruit of the Spirit, Holiness, speaking in heavenly tongues, God's Angels, agreement, and so on, what's your weapon of choice? I ask this because it's important to know what's in your Spiritual Arsenal. **Arsenal**: a place where weapons and military equipment are stored or made; an array of resources available for a certain purpose. How can you be effective at Spiritual warfare if you don't know your weapons, grace, and how to use them? King David was a man who knew his weapons and the grace of God that was on him to be effective at defeating his enemies. **Grace**: God's ability to do or get done what you cannot do in your strength or human ability. Here's a great example of why it's important to know how to use your weapons and grace and not somebody else's.

26 And David spake to the men that stood by him, saying, What shall be done to the man that killeth this Philistine, and taketh away the reproach from Israel? for who is this uncircumcised Philistine, that he should defy the armies of the living God? 27 And the people answered him after this manner, saying, So shall it be done to the man that killeth him.

28 And Eliab his eldest brother heard when he spake unto the men; and Eliab's anger was kindled against David, and he said, Why camest thou down hither? and with whom hast thou left those few sheep in the wilderness? I know thy pride, and the naughtiness of thine heart; for thou art come down that thou mightest see the battle. 29 And David said, What have I now done? Is there not a cause? 30 And he turned from him toward another, and spake after the same manner: and the people answered him again after the former manner. 31 And when the words were heard which David spake, they rehearsed them before Saul: and he sent for him. 32 And David said to Saul, Let no man's heart fail because of him; thy servant will go and fight with this Philistine. 33 And Saul said to David, Thou art not able to go against this Philistine to fight with him: for thou art but a youth, and he a man of war from his youth. 34 And David said unto Saul, Thy servant kept his father's sheep, and there came a lion, and a bear, and took a lamb out of the flock: 35 And I went out after him, and smote him, and delivered it out of his mouth: and when he arose against me, I caught him by his beard, and smote him, and slew him. 36 Thy servant slew both the lion and the bear: and this uncircumcised Philistine shall be as one of them, seeing he hath defied the armies of the living God. 37 David said moreover, The Lord that delivered me out of the paw of the lion, and out of the paw of the bear, he will deliver me out of the hand of this Philistine. And Saul said unto David, Go, and the Lord be with thee. 38 And Saul armed David with his armour, and he put an helmet of brass upon his head; also he armed him with a coat of mail. 39 And David girded his sword upon his armour, and he assayed to go; for he had not proved it. And David said unto Saul, I cannot go with these; for I have not proved them. And David put them off him. 40 And he took his staff in his hand, and chose him five smooth stones out of the brook, and put them in a shepherd's bag which he had, even in a scrip; and his sling was in his hand: and he drew near to the Philistine. 41 And the Philistine came on and drew near unto David; and the man that bare the shield went before him. 42 And when the Philistine looked about, and saw David, he disdained him: for he was but a youth, and ruddy, and of a fair countenance. 43 And the Philistine said unto David, Am I a dog, that thou comest to me with staves? And the Philistine cursed David by his gods. 44 And the Philistine said to David, Come to me, and I will give thy flesh unto the fowls of the air, and to the beasts of the field. 45 Then said David to the Philistine, Thou comest to me with a sword, and with a spear, and with a shield: but I come to thee in the name of the Lord of hosts, the God of the armies of Israel, whom thou hast defied. 46 This day will the Lord deliver thee into mine hand; and I will smite thee, and take thine head from thee; and I will give the carcases of the host of the Philistines this day unto the fowls of the air, and to the wild beasts of the earth; that all the earth may know that there is a God in Israel. 47 And all this assembly shall know that the Lord saveth not with sword and spear: for the battle is the Lord's, and he will give you into our hands. 48 And it came to pass, when the Philistine arose, and came, and drew nigh to meet David, that David hastened, and ran toward the army to meet the Philistine. 49 And David put his hand in his bag, and took thence a stone, and slang it, and smote the Philistine in his forehead, that the stone sunk into his forehead; and he fell upon his face to the earth. 50 So David prevailed over the Philistine with a sling and with a stone, and smote the Philistine, and slew him; but there was no sword in the hand of David. 51 Therefore David ran, and stood upon the Philistine, and took his sword, and drew it out of the sheath thereof, and slew him, and cut off his head therewith. And when the Philistines saw their champion was dead, they fled. **1Samuel 17:26-51**

Here are some of the lessons I would like to point out from those verses.

Verse 26 Lesson: there's payment/ reward that comes with going to war and winning. What will you gain?

verse 33 Lesson: do not allow people unqualified opinion tell you you're unqualified or stop you from doing that which you know God has equipped or told you to do because David didn't.

verse 36 lesson: David allowed God to teach and train him in private so he could be ready for public victory. It didn't matter how big the problem appeared in the flesh he knew the same training still applied. Stop allowing what it looks like in the natural make you question and doubt what God has equipped you with.

Verse 37 lesson: just because the circumstance change doesn't mean God did, He still the same God.

Verse 38 lesson: don't allow people to put their armor or ways of doing things on you. Even if y'all have the same weapons that doesn't mean y'all can use it the same way. Kindly tell them I don't fit your armor

Verse 39 lesson: Stand in your Grace with boldness, knowing you've been equipped by God.

Verse 40 lesson: use what works for you, your grace, your weapons assigned by God to you.

Verses 42 & 43 lesson: It's ok let them sleep on you because of your age, how you look, what you got on, and so on, you still qualified by God to get the job done.

Verses 45 & 46 lesson: Remember although you reap payment/rewards this is all about God's purpose and will being done, and God getting the glory. It's God's glory that makes us look good so never and I mean never let it go to your head like it's your doing vs God doing it through you.

It's important to stay humble after and during victory because pride comes for everybody it comes to make you fall. **Proverb 16:18** *pride goeth before destruction and a haughty spirit before a fall.*

Verse 47 lesson: don't be afraid to use your weapon because it's the Lord's battle anyway, and He choose how he wants to use you to win His battle. And yes, He chooses the foolish things that no flesh shall get the Glory. *27 But God hath chosen the foolish things of the world to confound the wise; and God hath chosen the weak things of the world to confound the things which are mighty; 28 And base things of the world, and things which are despised, hath God chosen, yea, and things which are not, to bring to nought things that are: 29 That no flesh should glory in his presence* **1Corintians 1:27-29.**

Verse 48 lesson: when are we as the believers of the True and Living God going to make haste or be hype to run and fight the battles God assigned to us?

Verses 49 & 50 lesson: David won the battle / got the victory because He did it God's way and not his own way or others. By using God grace and the weapons God trained him with in private.

If you can listen and follow God's instructions in private, then you're ready for public victory. It's through following God's instructions (not neglecting the details) that He trains and prepare us to know how to fight, war effectively in the Spirit realm to produce results, be victorious and succeed. Are you ready to war and do it God's way?

10

Part 2: Using your Weapons, the Right way

When choosing your weapon of war, one must know what way God has graced them to war. Whether you're starting out or been doing it for a while, asking God to reveal your weapons to you will help you in being effective. Sometimes you will have to try different weapons to see what suits you best or use weapons you don't want to. There's not one set way God reveals thing to us. So, whether it's you asking and Him speaking verbally or through seeing, trying out different weapons, word of knowledge or wisdom coming through Gods servant, you don't pick how God wants to make it known to you or what weapon or weapons He arms you with. So, don't complain or compare because it's not about you but how God desires to use you. And if you yield to God's leading you will see God knows what He is doing and He knows what it takes or what needs to be done to get the job done. Let God be God.

Whatever is your weaponry it will take learning, applying/putting into practice to make you a better warrior for the kingdom of God. As well there are levels of advancement or always room for you to grow. So don't get comfortable with doing it one way.

Here is a list of Spiritual weapons, there are more but I will name a few and speak on some of the ways they can be used: **Clapping of hands, Praise, Trust, walking the floor, Holiness, sword of the**

Spirit/ word of God, full amor of God, prayer, love, fruit of the Spirit/God character, obedience, watchmen, shofar, musical instruments, faith, Angles, tongues and more.

Clapping of hands- can be used in many ways. When one uses this weapon, it releases different sounds. Such as victory, agreement, praise, break things up, attack, encouragement and more. Clapping pairs well with dancing, praise, tongues, prayer, speaking the word of Truth and more. This weapon can be used in many ways so if this is your weapon make sure you ready to use it right. *O clap your hands, all ye people; shout unto God with the voice of triumph.* **Psalms 47:1.** *Blessed be the Lord my strength which teacheth my hands to war, and my fingers to fight:* **Psalms 144:1.**

Praise: So much can be said about how Praise can be used as a weapon. This is a special weapon for many reasons, one it's available to all God's people, two this is one of the weapons when used right will cause God Himself to come to you. *But thou art holy, O thou that inhabitest the praises of Israel.* **Psalms 22:3.** The Bible provides plenty examples of how God people would Praise God and their enemies would be defeated. *21 And when he had consulted with the people, he appointed singers unto the Lord, and that should praise the beauty of holiness, as they went out before the army, and to say, Praise the Lord; for his mercy endureth for ever. 22 And when they began to sing and to praise, the Lord set ambushments against the children of Ammon, Moab, and mount Seir, which were come against Judah; and they were smitten. 23 For the children of Ammon and Moab stood up against the inhabitants of mount Seir, utterly to slay and destroy them: and when they had made an end of the inhabitants of Seir, every one helped to destroy another. 24 And when Judah came toward the watch tower in the wilderness, they looked unto the multitude, and, behold, they were dead bodies fallen to the earth, and none escaped. 25 And when Jehoshaphat and his people came to take away the spoil of them, they found among them in abundance both riches with the dead bodies, and precious jewels, which they stripped off for* *themselves, more than they could carry away: and they were three days in gathering of the spoil, it was so much.* **2Chronicles 20: 21- 25**

If you going to use this weapon, make sure you praise God right and well (Hallelujah). *I will bless the Lord at all times: his praise shall continually be in my mouth. 2 My soul shall make her boast in the Lord: the humble shall hear thereof, and be glad. 3 O magnify the Lord with me, and let us exalt his name together* **Psalm** **34: 1-3**. This weapon pairs well with holiness, prayer, fasting, clapping, worship, the word of Truth and more. *But ye are a chosen generation, a royal priesthood, an holy nation, a peculiar people; that ye should shew forth the praises of him who hath called you out of darkness into his marvellous light;* **1Peter2:9**.

Full armor of God: Just as well one must know how to use their weapon/ offense, you must know how to play defense/armor up. defense: The action of defending from or resisting attack. This is Righteous warfare, so we don't play offense or defense how the world or normal people think. We do it the way that appears to be foolish (God's way) to the natural/ **carnal mind**: man's way of thinking, human reasoning. We war in the Spirit and not in the flesh, so Fleshly tactics weaken us in the Spirit Realm, and they don't work and work against us. **Flesh:** the fallen/ sin nature of man apart from God; the contaminated version of man. Again, one must be right (righteous before God to be most effective) going in or engaging in the Spirit/Heavenly realms. If not, there are consequences, like being or operating in the wrong spirit and realm. When this happens, you switch sides. Thanks be to God who protect us through us following His guidelines / instructions/ word of God and He give us His armor ☺. *10 Finally, my brethren, be strong in the Lord, and in the power of his might. 11 Put on the whole armour of God, that ye may be able to stand against the wiles of the devil. 12 For we wrestle not against flesh and blood, but against principalities, against powers, against the rulers of the darkness of this world, against spiritual wickedness in high places. 13 Wherefore take unto you the whole armour of God, that ye may be able to withstand in the evil day, and having done all, to stand. 14 Stand therefore, having your loins girt about with truth,* *and having on the breastplate of righteousness; 15 And your feet shod with the preparation of the gospel of peace; 16 Above all, taking the shield of faith, wherewith ye shall be able to quench all the fiery darts of the wicked. 17 And take the helmet of salvation, and the sword of the Spirit, which is the word of God: 18 Praying always with all prayer and supplication in the Spirit and watching thereunto with all perseverance and supplication for all saints;* **Ephesians 6:10 –18.**

Musical instruments: When this weapon is used right, they release a sound unto God that causes Him to come to your aid and war on your behalf. Musical instruments are also great for shifting the atmosphere and gives room for God or His presence to come in. Here are two examples of man and woman using instruments as their weapon.

14 But the Spirit of the Lord departed from Saul, and an evil spirit from the Lord troubled him. 15 And Saul's servants said unto him, Behold now, an evil spirit from God troubleth thee. 16 Let our lord now command thy servants, which are before thee, to seek out a man, who is a cunning player on an harp: and it shall come to pass, when the evil spirit from God is upon thee, that he shall play with his hand, and thou shalt be well. 17 And Saul said unto his servants, Provide me now a man that can play well, and bring him to me. 18 Then answered one of the servants, and said, Behold, I have seen a son of Jesse the Bethlehemite, that is cunning in playing, and a mighty valiant man, and a man of war, and prudent in matters, and a comely person, and the Lord is with him. 19 Wherefore Saul sent messengers unto Jesse, and said, Send me David thy son, which is with the sheep. 20 And Jesse took an ass laden with bread, and a bottle of wine, and a kid, and sent them by David his son unto Saul. 21 And David came to Saul, and stood before him: and he loved him greatly; and he became his armourbearer. 22 And Saul sent to Jesse, saying, Let David, I pray thee, stand before me; for he hath found favour in my sight. 23 And it came to pass, when the evil spirit from God was upon Saul, that David took an harp, and played with his hand: so Saul was refreshed, and was well, and the evil spirit departed from him **1Samuel 16:14-23**. The harp instrument being used the right way was able to shift the atmosphere, war off the evil spirit, and bring peace.

Second example: *And Miriam the prophetess, the sister of Aaron, took a timbrel in her hand; and all the women went out after her with timbrels and with dances* **Exodus15:20**

Here's an example of a different musical instrument the timbrel or also known as tambourine. Which was paired with dancing and people/ agreement (There is power in **agreement**.) Whatever your musical instrument, perfect and use it right and you will see the fruit/results.

Love: One of the strongest weapons one can have and it's available to everyone. This was the weapon Jesus used to reconcile us back to God (*For God so loved the world, that he gave his only begotten Son, that whosoever believeth in him should not perish, but have everlasting life.* **John 3:16**;) and take back the keys of death and hell. *I am he that liveth, and was dead; and, behold, I am alive for evermore, Amen; and have the keys of hell and of death.* **Revelation 1:18.** Love is so powerful because it's God himself. Using this weapon right is a must/ necessity of life. This is one of the things that happen when Love is used right. 😊

17 Recompense to no man evil for evil. Provide things honest in the sight of all men. 18 If it be possible, as much as lieth in you, live peaceably with all men. 19 Dearly beloved, avenge not yourselves, but rather give place unto wrath: for it is written, Vengeance is mine; I will repay, saith the Lord. 20 Therefore if thine enemy hunger, feed him; if he thirst, give him drink: for in so doing thou shalt heap coals of fire on his head. 21 Be not overcome of evil, but overcome evil with good. **Roman 12:17-21**

Word of God/ Sword of the Spirt/ Word of Truth: Everything is predicated by this weapon the **Word of God**. It's A sustainer of life. *And he humbled thee, and suffered thee to hunger, and fed thee with manna, which thou knewest not, neither did thy fathers know; that he might make thee know that man doth not live by bread only, but by every word that proceedeth out of the mouth of the Lord doth man live.* **Deuteronomy 8:3. The** word of God produce our faith, salvation, belief system, principles, life, how we war, protection, strength, it's our sword in the Spirit and more. *For the word of God is quick, and powerful, and sharper than any twoedged sword, piercing even to the dividing asunder of soul and spirit, and of the joints and marrow, and is a discerner of the thoughts and intents of the heart*

Hebrews 4:12. One must be skilled to use this weapon; warning this weapon is not to be handle careless or it can cut you. This weapon takes practice in yielding to the Spirit of the Lord, studying, and rightly dividing the word of Truth. *Study to shew thyself approved unto God, a workman that needeth not to be ashamed, rightly dividing the word of truth* **2Timothy 2:15.** This weapon pairs well with all the weapons especially faith, prayer and worship.

Holiness and Fruit of God Spirit/Character: When Holiness and the Character of God are your weapons your lifestyle becomes a weapon. Meaning the way you live your life before God becomes a defense and offense against the kingdom of darkness. *13 Then certain of the vagabond Jews, exorcists, took upon them to call over them which had evil spirits the name of the Lord Jesus, saying, We adjure you by Jesus whom Paul preacheth. 14 And there were seven sons of one Sceva, a Jew, and chief of the priests, which did so. 15 And the evil spirit answered and said, Jesus I know, and Paul I know; but who are ye? 16 And the man in whom the evil spirit was leaped on them, and overcame them, and prevailed against them, so that they fled out of that house naked and wounded.* **Acts 19: 13-16.** When you live right the spirit realm bows to the God in you because it's automatic for them to respond to God. I mentioned how there are rules that govern the Spirit and earthly/natural realms; as well there are rankings in the Spirit and earthly realms. **Rank:** a position that describe or distinguish one authority and or power. No one ranks higher than God not in the natural/ earthly or Spirit realm. The kingdom of darkness bows, flee and surrender to God. *28 And when he was come to the other side into the country of the Gergesenes, there met him two possessed with devils, coming out of the tombs, exceeding fierce, so that no man might pass by that way. 29 And, behold, they cried out, saying, What have we to do with thee, Jesus, thou Son of God? art thou come* *hither to torment us before the time?* **Matthew 8: 28-29.** These weapons make every weapon more powerful and pairs well with faith, praise, the word of God. *3 Who shall ascend into the hill of the Lord? or who shall stand in his holy place? 4 He that hath clean hands, and a pure heart; who hath not lifted up his soul unto vanity, nor sworn deceitfully* **Psalm 24:4.** One cannot ascend or last/ live in the presence of God or high realms in the Spirit without a clean heart, purity, holiness and a change in nature/fruit of God Spirit/God character or nature. *He that dwelleth in the secret place of the most High shall abide under the shadow of the Almighty* **Psalm 91:1.**

Wisdom: Wisdom as a weapon is a must. It takes more than power to win a war. Wisdom gives you the how to, strategy, and insight to not only win but how to use what you have skillfully. *13 This wisdom have I seen also under the sun, and it seemed great unto me: 14 There was a little city, and few men within it; and there came a great king against it, and besieged it, and built great bulwarks against it: 15 Now there was found in it a poor wise man, and he by his wisdom delivered the city; yet no man remembered that same poor man. 16 Then said I, Wisdom is better than strength: nevertheless the poor man's wisdom is despised, and his words are not heard. 17 The words of wise men are heard in quiet more than the cry of him that ruleth among fools. 18 Wisdom is better than weapons of war: but one sinner destroyeth much good.* **Ecclesiastes 9: 13-18** Wisdom pairs well with all weapons.

Walking the floor, Speaking in Tongues, and Prayer: These three are a dangerous combination/weapons to the kingdom of darkness when used correctly. Walking the floor stir up the gifts, helps it to flow fluently, and is used prophetically/symbolically in the Spirit realm. *Every place that the sole of your foot shall tread upon, that have I given unto you, as I said unto Moses* **Joshua 1:3.** Speaking in Tongues/ heavenly language allows us to easily penetrate the Spirit realms, speak directly to God in a language the enemy cannot hear, allows the Holy Spirit to pray through us, and war in the Spirit and more. *For he that speaketh in an unknown tongue speaketh not unto men, but unto God: for* *no man understandeth him; howbeit in the spirit he speaketh mysteries* **1Corinthians 14:2.** Prayer can be used in so many ways but when it comes to using it with fervency it becomes a weapon. *Confess your faults one to another, and pray one for another, that ye may be healed. The effectual fervent prayer of a righteous man availeth much. 17 Elias was a man subject to like passions as we are, and he prayed earnestly that it might not rain: and it rained not on the earth by the space of three years and six months. 18 And he prayed again, and the heaven gave rain, and the earth brought forth her fruit* **James 5:16-18.** When you use all three weapons together watch out and know what you are doing!

Angels: it's one thing to have the help of another believer but when you got the help of Angels is a game/war changer. When God/ the Lord of Host sends His Angels as weapons to help us He is sending Supernatural aid or assistance to us. *5 Peter therefore was kept in prison: but prayer was made without ceasing of the church unto God for him. 6 And when Herod would have brought him forth, the same night Peter was sleeping between two soldiers, bound with two chains: and the keepers before the door kept the prison. 7 And, behold, the angel of the Lord came upon him, and a light shined in the prison: and he smote Peter on the side, and raised him up, saying, Arise up quickly. And his chains fell off from his hands. 8 And the angel said unto him, Gird thyself, and bind on thy sandals. And so he did. And he saith unto him, Cast thy garment about thee, and follow me. 9 And he went out, and followed him; and wist not that it was true which was done by the angel; but thought he saw a vision. 10 When they were past the first and the second ward, they came unto the iron gate that leadeth unto the city; which opened to them of his own accord: and they went out, and passed on through one street; and forthwith the angel departed from him. 11 And when Peter was come to himself, he said, Now I know of a surety, that the Lord hath sent his angel, and hath delivered me out of the hand of Herod, and from all the expectation of the people of the Jews* **Acts 12:5-11.** This weapon pairs well with faith and prayer.

Watchmen and Shofar/Ram's Horn: When it comes to warfare these are two must have weapons. A watchmen see in the Spirit and can help guard, warn, block, see what's coming, keep safe and more. *Son of man, I have made thee a watchman unto the house of Israel: therefore hear the word at my mouth, and give them warning from me* **Ezekiel 3:17.** The shofar/rams horn can be used in multiple ways but when needed as a weapon one has to be skilled to release the sound for warring or victory. *2 And the Lord said unto Joshua, See, I have given into thine hand Jericho, and the king thereof, and the mighty men of valour. 3 And ye shall compass the city, all ye men of war, and go round about the city once. Thus shalt thou do six days. 4 And seven priests shall bear before the ark seven trumpets of rams' horns: and the seventh day ye shall compass the city seven times, and the priests shall blow with the trumpets. 5 And it shall come to pass, that when they make a long blast with the ram's horn, and when ye hear the sound of the trumpet, all the people shall shout with a great shout; and the wall of the city shall fall down flat, and the people shall ascend up every man straight before him* **Joshua 6:2-5.** This weapon pairs well with praise and dancing.

Trust: When one has the confidence in Knowing God will do what He or His word said it becomes a weapon against the kingdom of darkness. *And such as do wickedly against the covenant shall he corrupt by flatteries: but the people that do know their God shall be strong and do exploits* **Daniel 11:32.** Most people won't wait on God because trusting Him is not an easy thing to do it takes practice but yields great rewards. *3 Thou wilt keep him in perfect peace, whose mind is stayed on thee: because he trusteth in thee. 4 Trust ye in the Lord for ever: for in the Lord Jehovah is everlasting strength:* **Isaiah 26:3-4.** This weapon pairs well with faith, the word of God and love.

Faith and Obedience: All the weapons fall or rest on these two weapons Faith and Obedience. These two goes hand in hand because you can be skilled in handling your weapon but if you don't believe and step out and use it/ follow God's instructions you will not produce any result, or your weapon is wasted. How many people reading this right now has Spiritual weapons and not operating in faith and obedience to God with it? *For as the body without the spirit is dead, so faith without works is dead also* **James 2:26.** We all believe in something, but the question is, are we believing in the right thing/ word of God? *So then faith cometh by hearing, and hearing by the word of God* **Romans 10:17.** If you don't believe then you will not be effective, have power, or you'll be using the weapons or warring in vain. When it comes to obedience there is no replacement. *And Samuel said, Hath the Lord as great delight in burnt offerings and sacrifices, as in obeying the voice of the Lord? Behold, to obey is better than sacrifice, and to hearken than the fat of rams* **1Samuel 15:22.** Doing things God way is a must, we cannot be effective without Obedience.

No more overlooking your treasures/weapons; seeing and thinking as God do is a must. There is a war to be won and it will not be won in the flesh but the Spirit. *8 For my thoughts are not your thoughts, neither are your ways my ways, saith the Lord. 9 For as the heavens are higher than the earth, so are my ways higher than your ways, and my thoughts than your thoughts* **Isaiah 55: 8-9.**

11

Let's War: its War Time

Too many battles or wars have been and are being lost because we are trying to fight a spiritual war in the natural/flesh. *3 For though we walk in the flesh, we do not war after the flesh: 4 (For the weapons of our warfare are not carnal, but mighty through God to the pulling down of strong holds;) 5 Casting down imaginations, and every high thing that exalteth itself against the knowledge of God, and bringing into captivity every thought to the obedience of Christ;* **2 Corinthians 10:3-5**. It's through the Spirit of God we war, get things done, fulfill the will of God, victories and so on. There's power in knowing how to rest, rely, and dwell in the Spirit of God. *Then he answered and spake unto me, saying, This is the word of the Lord unto Zerubbabel, saying, Not by might, nor by power, but by my spirit, saith the Lord of hosts* **Zechariah 4:6**. Surrendering our will to God and Submitting to God will is how we win. Satan know this so he strives to keep us in our flesh (emotion, your will, human reasoning, sin, being petty and so on) this is how he win.

The purpose of this book is to teach you how to be a righteous warrior in God's kingdom. This starts with one coming into the righteousness of God through Jesus Christ and then learning to war God's way and following God's rules. There is no being effective doing things outside the realm of the Spirit/God.

4 That the righteousness of the law might be fulfilled in us, who walk not after the flesh, but after the Spirit. 5 For they that are after the flesh do mind the things of the flesh; but they that are after the Spirit the things of the Spirit. 6 For to be carnally minded is death; but to be spiritually minded is life and peace. 7 Because the carnal mind is enmity against God: for it is not subject to the law of God, neither indeed can be. 8 So then they that are in the flesh cannot please God **Romans 8:4-8.**

The righteousness of God cannot be done or fulfilled walking or living in the flesh. It takes living in and obeying the Holy Spirit that brings us into right standing/ being right with God. This is not I repeat this is not something we can do by ourselves. One can say they believe or have faith in Jesus or God, but if you do not obey Him, Holy Spirit, His word then something is wrong and off with your faith/ belief system. God does not want us worshiping Him with our lips and our hearts being detached from Him. *This people draweth nigh unto me with their mouth, and honoureth me with their lips; but their heart is far from me.* **Matthew 15:8** This is a quick way to become religious.

When a person is walking after the flesh, they are not looking to please God or follow His rules; they are doing whatever is going to satisfy the flesh. *For the flesh lusteth against the Spirit, and the Spirit against the flesh: and these are contrary the one to the other: so that ye cannot do the things that ye would Galatians* **5:17.** We are our most powerful selves when we are in the Spirit of God, but if Satan can keep us in the flesh, then we lose. It's the job of the flesh/sin nature to work or want different than the Holy Spirit/ nature of God, it becomes very easy for the enemy/ Satan to control, manipulate, and deceive the flesh (emotions, mind and will). If one can overcome their flesh by yielding and living in the Spirit, you can overcome the enemy and get victory every time. This is how we war effectively. To make this very simple being in the Spirit of God = countless victories. Being in the flesh = countless defeats/ loses and death. It cost too much to be in the flesh.

12

Reference Page

"**Wimps**" https://www.merriam-webster.com/dictionary/wimp
"**Defense**" https://www.dictionary.com/browse/defense
"**Offense**" https://www.dictionary.com/browse/offense
"**Arsenal**" https://www.dictionary.com/browse/arsenal
All other definitions are giving by inspiration of the Holy Spirit of God.

www.ingramcontent.com/pod-product-compliance
Lightning Source LLC
Chambersburg PA
CBHW072210100526
44589CB00015B/2463